FIRST, LEARN TO PRACTICE

by Tom Heany

First published by Dog Ear Publishing
4010 W. 86th Street, Ste H
Indianapolis, IN 46268
www.dogearpublishing.net

ISBN: 978-1-4575-0775-5

This book is printed on acid-free paper.

Printed in the United States of America

To Gloria.

Table of Contents

GOOD HABITS

TOOLS

NOT THE END

GETTING STARTED

No one ever tells you how to practice. They all say, "If you want to be any good, you have to practice." But they never tell you how.

This book is about how *I* practice. Practicing is different for everybody, and there are certainly other approaches; this is what works for me. The ideas in this book have helped make my practice enjoyable and effective. Whether you're a beginner or a life-long player, they can show you how to get more out of the time you devote to practicing.

You may think practice is boring and painful and, sad to say, that's the experience many people have had. But it doesn't have to be. In fact, when you do it right, it's satisfying, interesting, invigorating and, most important of all, enjoyable. Like playing, practicing is a creative activity. It's worth mastering. It makes you feel good. It's fun.

But no one is born knowing how to practice. Just as with any other skill, you first have to learn how, and then you have to do it for a while until you can do it well. The better you get, the more you enjoy it. And one of the most important concepts in this book – one of the seven Big Ideas – is this:

If you don't enjoy your practicing, change it until you do.

Unfortunately, too many of us learn about practicing by having music lessons forced on us as children. We remember a lot of "Play this five times," "Memorize this scale," "You have to practice for half an hour *every day*" and "Don't ask why. You'll thank me later." We remember musical exercises that seemed difficult, pointless and meaningless, and had nothing to do with anything we thought of as music. And, of course, we remember how lonely it was to sit all alone for half an hour every day. It's like being sent to the corner. To a child, this type of practicing is not enjoyable – it's punishment. Who could possibly enjoy that?

But that same child who fidgets and squirms through 30 minutes on the piano bench (and not a second more) will then run outside with a basketball and shoot layup after layup trying to get it just right. Isn't that practicing, too?

So, why is practicing basketball fun for this boy, and practicing piano torture? Well, when he's practicing basketball:

- He's interested.

- He's in control.

- He wants to be there.

- He enjoys all the motions he's going through.

- He has instant feedback on every shot – he knows immediately whether he's succeeded (the ball goes in) or not.

- He has immediate satisfaction with every success.

- He's imagining himself to be better than he is – in fact, he's probably pretending to be the best basketball player he can think of.

Who wouldn't enjoy that? And can we make piano practice more like basketball practice?

What exactly is practicing? Hard to say, because it's different for everyone. There are elements that belong in every practice routine – like repetition, commitment, consistency, listening and, again, enjoyment. On the other hand, we each have distinct personalities, goals, standards, schedules and tastes, and all of those affect how we practice, when we practice, what we practice and how much we practice. Some players will practice four hours a day; some will aim for an hour a day and only get in 45 minutes. Some will concentrate on scales, arpeggios and theory; some will just play songs. Some want to play at Lincoln Center; some want to play at church.

Let's sidestep the idea of *defining* practicing and, instead, *describe* it. Here's the description I have found most helpful, and the one I come back to repeatedly in FIRST, LEARN TO PRACTICE:

> *Practicing is searching for and mastering the ideal motions necessary to play music.*

Like everything, practicing can be described in more than one way:

> *Practicing is developing and maintaining ear-hand coordination.*

> *Practicing is learning how to listen.*

> *Practicing is repetition with purpose.*

But there's a more important question than "What is practicing?" That question is "Why practice?" Again, there's no single answer, but here are a few good ones:

> *I practice so that I'll become a better musician.*

> *I practice so that I'll have more fun when I play.*

> *I practice because I enjoy practicing.*

3

I practice so I'll sound my best when I perform.

I practice because it makes me a better person.

(Surprised at the last one? The pianist and teacher Seymour Bernstein has said this may be the most important reason to practice, and I won't argue with him.)

Here's why "Why?" is important. Practicing requires a lot of time and energy and, the more you want to accomplish, the more time and energy you'll need. At some point, when you have invested more time and energy than you ever thought possible, you'll be working on something very tricky and you'll look up at the ceiling and ask yourself, "Why, exactly, am I doing this?" When that happens, it's good to have an answer.

Knowing the "why" will also help you decide "what", "when" and "how." For example, if you're practicing to get ready for a performance, you may feel you need a few hours a day every day working on the specific pieces you'll be performing. If you're practicing because you just want to be a better musician, you may find 30 minutes of theory in the morning and 30 minutes of technique in the evening do the trick for you. If you just want to be able to play a few old favorite songs with friends, 15 minutes every other day may be enough.

FIRST, LEARN TO PRACTICE is part philosophy and part nuts-and-bolts. It describes ideas, attitudes, approaches and techniques that will help you practice better, and as a result, play better. Most of these can be expressed in a sentence:

Don't worry about the hard parts.

Be optimistic.

Make music.

Fourteen of the ideas come up often enough that they receive special emphasis (Seven Big Ideas and Seven Good Habits). You may look at some of them and ask, "How is that even possible?", but don't worry; think of them as targets. Most of the value in a target is not hitting it, but aiming at it.

The reason for using sayings is that they're easy to remember. When you're practicing, you have a lot of things to pay attention to. You don't need complicated theories about how to practice getting in your way. But sayings like "Go slow" and "Be Optimistic" are easy to remember. And, as simple as they are, any one of them can change your practicing and your playing.

Most of the ideas in FIRST, LEARN TO PRACTICE come from my own experience practicing guitar and piano (and occasionally mandolin and fiddle and, for about twenty minutes in 1988, flute) over more years than I can count. In 2004 and 2005 I conducted dozens of interviews with guitar, bass, drum and keyboard teachers for the National Guitar Workshop. I asked each of them about practicing, among many other things, and learned a great deal from their thoughtful and generous answers. And when I lived in New York I studied with Myron Weiss. His thinking about music, guitar-playing and practicing is still inspiring to me twenty years later.

You can read the sections of this book in any order. You can read the whole book from front to back, or you can read a page at random each time you sit down to practice. You can start trying out the ideas in the book before you finish reading it if you want, and you can try bits and pieces of it without having to apply everything in it at once.

You'll notice that some of the ideas in the book come up over and over; learning, like practicing, involves a lot of repetition. You'll also notice that there isn't too much music notation. This is, after all, a book about practicing, not a book about music.

So, to return to a question from a few pages back: Is it possible to make practicing piano – or violin, oboe, saxophone or accordion– more like practicing basketball? Is it possible to enjoy practicing?

Absolutely! That's what this book is about.

THE FIRST BIG IDEA

If you're not enjoying your practicing, change it until you are.

Let's talk about the boy from the last chapter, who flees the piano bench after 30 minutes of torture so that he can shoot layups until it's too dark to see the basket. Why does he enjoy practicing basketball so much when he doesn't enjoy practicing piano at all?

Here are a few reasons:

1. <u>Control</u> - he's practicing because he wants to practice, and he's making all the decisions about what to do himself. He starts when he wants to, and he stops when he wants to.

2. <u>Movement</u> – All that running, jumping and shooting is exhilarating, whether he's good at it or not so good.

3. <u>Feedback</u> – when the ball goes in, he knows immediately that he's had a success.

4. <u>Satisfaction</u> – every basket is satisfying. Even shots that miss are satisfying if the moves (left hand, off the backboard, eyes closed) feel good.

5. <u>Emotion</u> – he's excited just to be outdoors and active; he's thrilled when the ball goes in and crushed when it doesn't.

6. <u>Imagination</u> – he's imagining himself as the greatest player he can think of. What's more, he believes it's possible for him to become that good a player himself.

7. <u>Identity</u> – it makes him feel like something he wants to be – a basketball player – whether, again, he's good or not so good.

If practicing the piano, the violin, the trumpet or the flute were more like that, we'd have more Van Cliburns, Mark O'Connors, Wynton Marsalises and James Galways.

But it can be like that, and this is very good news, because if you want to play music well, you're going to spend a lot of time practicing. In fact, you could easily spend more time practicing than you do playing. It would be a terrible waste to spend all that time doing something that you don't enjoy. And if you enjoy your practicing, you'll practice more often, practice longer and practice better. Your playing will advance farther and faster. You'll have more fun and get more done.

Getting back to the kid with the basketball: let's see what we can learn from him. How can we make our practicing more enjoyable, like his?

The differences between his two practices are mostly mental. All of the following statements apply to basketball but not piano – for him, at least:

He's in charge. He decides what to do and what to pay attention to; he alone evaluates what he's done; he decides when to start and when to stop; he accepts blame when things go wrong and assigns himself credit when things go right.

He's working with movement. His concentration is on running, jumping, spinning, dribbling and shooting, trying to do each one better. And he's not just thinking about it – he's feeling it, too, and it's exhilarating. He enjoys movement for its own sake.

He has his own goals. Short term, he's trying to put the ball in; long term, he's trying to become the next Kobe Bryant (and he believes he can).

He gets instant feedback. With every shot he knows right away if he succeeded or failed; he doesn't have to wait for his weekly lesson to find out.

His emotions and his imagination are working for him.

What he's doing matters to him. When he's practicing, he feels like a basketball player, which, at least in the moment, he wants to be. He believes it's good to be a basketball player, and he probably has friends and family members who agree that it's good for him to be a basketball player.

So, with him as our guide, how can we make our practicing more enjoyable?

Be in charge. Childhood practicing is *passive*. The teacher says, "Do this five times," or "Play this piece," and we do. Ask a child, "Why are you practicing that?", and she'll probably say, "Because my teacher told me to."

But most people get more pleasure out of what they do when they're *active*. So take hold of your practicing. Set a schedule, and stick to it Make a routine for yourself, and adjust it until it's perfect. Figure out what you need to work on and why. Then work on it, and notice when you get better at it. Take pleasure in the improvements you make. Write them down. (Your teacher can help, but remember: It's not lessons that make you better; it's practicing that makes you better.)

Focus on movement. There's great pleasure in working with your hands. Building model airplanes, knitting, cooking, making furniture, fixing cars, juggling, doing card tricks – people who do these things enjoy the sensation of doing them as much as they enjoy the outcome of doing them. Music is the same. Dorothy Taubman said, "When movements are correctly executed, the feeling is delicious." Later we'll get more deeply into the other reasons for focusing on movement, but for now, it's all about joy.

Goals. A big part of enjoyment, especially for adults, is satisfaction – feeling that we've accomplished something. Goals, both short term ("I'm going to play this scale through three octaves without pausing") and long term ("I'm going to perform three pieces at the family Christmas party") give forward motion to your practicing. They help you avoid two common practicing traps - doing the same thing over and over without getting any better, and fooling around with no direction. Both lead directly to boredom and frustration, just like childhood practicing.

Instant feedback. The best way to learn anything is to have instant feedback on whether you're doing it correctly or incorrectly. This lets you adjust in real time, and helps you avoid practicing mistakes. You get lots of immediate rewards when you do things right, and you improve faster. You have confidence in what you're doing – you're never wondering if maybe you're on the wrong track.

Most of us do not have anyone to watch us while we practice and give us this kind of feedback. We have to learn to do it ourselves. We'll talk about how to do it later, in the chapter on looping. For now, it's enough to say that you'll enjoy practicing more when you have frequent reminders that you're doing things right, and when you improve quickly.

Emotion and imagination. Each is a double-edged sword, but we're talking about enjoyment, so for now we'll only look at the good sides. Music is inherently emotional stuff. As much as we'll talk about movement and technique, music without emotion is just marks on paper. If you can tap into that emotion in your practicing you'll enjoy it more.

The same is true of imagination. Imagination is what makes it possible for you to set goals and challenge yourself. It lets you dream yourself into the Boston Symphony Orchestra or the Count Basie Band. Imagination will help you through the countless hours of repetition that is necessary (sorry!) to get better on your instrument.

Spending an hour with your emotions and your imagination fully engaged in music – what could be more enjoyable than that?

Meaning. Many of us who practice music as adults secretly ask ourselves, "Why am I still doing this? Shouldn't I have quit when I got out of school?" Or, "Isn't there something more important – work, family, home – that I should be doing instead of practicing?"

To enjoy practicing, you have to accept that it's right for you to practice. You are a musician – an amateur, perhaps, or a beginner, or a student, but still a musician. Music and musicians have been part of every human culture on earth since the beginning of human culture on earth. Music is valuable for its own sake, and it's valuable for what it does for you.

Decide how much time you can reasonably give it, whether that's fifteen minutes a day or eight hours a day. For that period of time, make it the most important thing on your agenda. Own it, value it, and enjoy it.

What else makes practicing enjoyable?

How about getting better at playing your instrument?

How about the increased personal growth that comes from active engagement in a disciplined, creative process over a long period of time? Admittedly most people who practice aren't doing it for the personal growth, but it's still very real. Practicing music actively and thoughtfully gets the brain firing on all cylinders: it involves touch, sight, hearing, motion, emotion, intellect, imagination, visualization and memory all at once – not to mention music. Practicing takes discipline, planning, commitment and concentration. And at the same time it's enjoyable and satisfying.

If at this point you're saying "My practicing is NOTHING AT ALL like that," don't worry. This is something to aim for, one piece at a time, and there are plenty of pieces yet to come. If you're a beginner, your hands may not have reached the point yet where doing it right feels "delicious." You may not be ready to take over the reins of practicing quite yet.

All you need to do, when you sit down to practice, is this – expect to enjoy it. Look for the things that you're already enjoying, and notice them – appreciate them – savor them - write them down so you remember them. In the beginning, you may find five or ten minutes out of thirty that you enjoy, and that will be enough. Over time you'll find more. Then, you'll be dissatisfied with the parts of practicing that you *don't* enjoy, and you'll change them. That's all it takes.

THE SECOND BIG IDEA

Practice movement – music will follow.

How do we make music?

We make music by moving our bodies – hands, fingers, arms, back, shoulders, legs, feet, breath – against an instrument. (When you sing, you don't have an instrument to move against; you *are* the instrument. But you still move your whole upper body to control your breath, and your mouth and throat to shape the sound.)

Picture yourself, instrument in hand, ready to play. What happens when you think to yourself, "Start playing now"?

Nothing.

Nothing happens until you use your body – fingers, hands, arms, feet, lips, or breath – to exert force on the instrument. It's not thinking that makes sound come out of the instrument; it's doing. It's moving. So movement is what we work on; in fact, it's really the only thing we can work on, since it's the only thing over which we have direct control. Think of it this way: *music is not what we do; music is the result of what we do.* We play music, but we practice movement.

This is a very basic, fundamental way of thinking about practicing, and it's not necessarily for everybody. Most people concentrate on higher-level ideas, like phrasing, or style, or expression. Those things are important, of course, and you have to spend time working on them. Just remember: none of them is possible without motion. All of them – phrasing, style, expression, timing – require movement. If you can't make your fingers do what you want them to, then you can't play with the phrasing you want; you can't play in the style you want; you can't convey the emotion you feel; you can't even play in time. Movement makes all the rest possible.

Remember our description of practicing from Chapter 1?

Practicing is searching for and mastering the ideal movements necessary to perform music.

Searching for ideal movements means noticing how we move when we play a piece of music and making sure that every move is smooth, relaxed, efficient and comfortable.

Some movements are easy to examine and control. It's easy to notice how your fingers are moving, for example, because you spend so much time looking at them. Other movements are fairly subtle and not so easy to notice. Sure you know what your fingers are doing, but what about your wrists? How about your shoulders? And are you holding your breath?

Some of the things we need to think about don't seem like movements at all – for example, how to hold the instrument (or the pick, or the sticks), or how to sit at a keyboard. Each of these things is the starting point for all our other movements. Every move a violinist makes with his bow is made possible by how he holds it. If he holds it the wrong way, he can't move it the right way. And posture affects everything - breathing, arm movement, hand movement, stamina, and, believe it or not, mental attitude.

As we find these ideal movements, we want our muscles to memorize them. Muscle memory comes with repetition. Fortunately, so does refinement. We don't have to jump from so-so movements to ideal movements in a single practice session. As we practice them, they become easier and more familiar. Our hands develop strength and flexibility that is specific to those movements. As long as we're paying attention, they move closer to the ideal we're aiming for.

Of course, if we're not paying attention, it's just as easy for muscles to memorize the wrong movement as the right movement. Suppose I decide to memorize a G scale by playing it over and over. And suppose, to make the time go quicker, I sit down to watch Judge Judy on TV while I do it. The more attention I pay to Judge Judy, the less I pay to my fingers, and the sloppier and less focused my movements become. Soon my fingers will have memorized sloppy and unfocused movements, and then I'll be stuck with them until I can unlearn them – not an easy thing to do.

Repetition is essential to practicing just about anything; unfortunately, it can be boring. Play a fragment of music over and over often enough and you stop hearing it; you tune it out, and your mind drifts away to what you had for lunch, or what your friends are doing while you're sitting here practicing. And when your mind drifts, your focus and attention drift away with it; once again, instead of teaching your muscles ideal movements, you're teaching them sloppy, careless movements.

Boredom is not the only culprit for this mid-practice drift. Oddly enough, the other is the thing that brought us here in the first place – music.

We're musicians, and music is always calling us. It's a very short step from practicing a piece of music that's hard, and needs work (and therefore sounds bad), to playing something we like better that's easy, and doesn't need work (and sounds a lot better). We drift away from the piece that needs repetition, and instead have fun fooling around with pieces that don't.

The problem in these instances is that we're focusing on music, when we should be focusing on movement. Make that one change, and everything else changes, too.

Focus on movement, and suddenly there's a lot to do during all those repetitions when the music has stopped sounding like music. Suddenly we're tracking what's happening in our fingers, wrists, shoulders, neck and back. We're making adjustments to correct mistakes or smooth out our motions. We're looking for the mechanical cause of each wrong note. Repetition has become active instead of passive.

Focus on movement, and immediately we're relying on our eyes much more than our ears. Visual input is much more precise than auditory input for most of us. We can describe, analyze and understand what we see more easily than what we hear.

Focus on movement, and our frame of mind becomes analytical. We start thinking less like artists and more like mechanics and, when it comes to practicing, that's a major step in the right direction.

Focus on movement, and we're dealing with something over which we have direct control. We can make a change and see the effect right away.

Focus on movement, and the enjoyment and satisfaction come from getting the moves right, not from hearing the music – from how it **feels**, not from how it **sounds**. Once the move feels right, we want to do it over and over to enjoy that feeling, not to wander off after the melody.

One last reason to practice movement: It doesn't matter how well you understand a piece if you can't play it. After all, you practice so that you can play music, not so that you can explain it. And playing is movement. When you can make the moves, you can make the music.

This brings us back to where we started:

Practice movement – music will follow.

We've emphasized movement and talked very little about music. This doesn't mean that music is unimportant, or that you shouldn't think about music when you practice. It just means that movement comes first.

If you want to be a baseball player, you first have to learn to throw a baseball. All the theory about curveballs and fastballs, sliders and change-ups – none of it matters if you can't throw the ball from the pitcher's mound to home plate. First things first. And if you want to play music, you first have to learn to move your hands a certain way. Music comes from movement.

The search for ideal movement is life-long. As long as you play, you'll need to keep at it. The hand-brain-eye-ear circuit is complicated and takes a lot of maintenance. As you get better, your body will change; it will be capable of more things, and more difficult things. Your improving ability will lead you to look for new, perhaps more challenging music to play, and that will lead to ever-higher standards for what constitutes 'ideal.' But that's half the fun.

THE THIRD BIG IDEA

Playing and Practicing are two different things.

What do you mean when you say, "I'm going to practice for a while"?

Each of us has his or her own unique answer to that question. For the moment, though, let's start with a very broad answer that covers everybody, and then narrow it down. Let's say that "I'm going to practice for a while" means "I'm going to spend some time with my instrument."

Now: when you are spending time with your instrument, there are many different things you can be doing, and practicing is only one off them. You might be:

- Playing
- Writing
- Learning
- Arranging
- Fooling Around
- Exploring
- Practicing

All are good, important things to do. They overlap each other a bit (you can learn while you practice, for example), and each can help you become a better musician. In fact, it would be hard to get anywhere without doing all of them.

But we're talking about practicing, and the first step towards improving your practicing is to identify it. We want the word 'practicing' to mean something specific. When you practice, we want it to be very clear that what you're doing is actually practicing and not something else.

Practicing is not just spending time with your instrument.

AND

Time spent with your instrument is not automatically practicing.

So far, we've said a little about what practicing isn't; now let's describe what it is. We've already described practicing as a search for ideal motion. We can also describe it as an attitude.

The great New York Knicks forward Bernard King was known for his 'game face,' an imposing scowl that let teammates, opponents and fans alike know that he had come to play and was dead serious about it.

But King's game face wasn't just an expression. It was the outward sign of the mental and physical attitude that he brought to every game. The qualities that opposing players read in King's face – intensity, determination, confidence, will power – came from the inside. You could say that his game face was his game.

FIRST, LEARN TO PRACTICE is about building your mental and physical attitude toward practicing. Ultimately, you'll see that your attitude *is* your practicing, just like Bernard King's game face was his game.

But what does that mean – 'your attitude is your practicing'? It means that what separates good practicing from bad practicing, enjoyable practicing from boring and tiresome practicing, your practicing from the guy next door's practicing, is what's happening in your head. Yes, we're practicing movement. Movement is our raw material. But our most important tools are mental. These are things like:

- What we pay attention to;

- What our standards are;

- What our goals are;

- Concentration;

- Optimism;

- Honesty; and

- Patience.

Practicing and Playing are as different as cooking and eating. In some ways they almost completely unrelated.

Playing music is an artistic, emotional activity. Ideally, you'd like to get your conscious mind out of the way as much as possible when you're playing – the less thinking and the more 'flow', the better.

Practicing is an analytical activity. It requires a completely different mental attitude. When you practice, you break things down into parts and study them. You look at everything – the music you're trying to learn, the movements of your fingers, the results you achieve, etc. – and try to understand how all the pieces work together. You have to think like a mechanic.

THE MECHANIC'S MINDSET

A mechanic works on an engine piece by piece. He tries to understand what each piece does, how each piece moves and how each piece interacts with each other piece. He investigates whether or not each piece is doing what it's supposed to be doing, and then he adjusts the pieces individually and together until everything is behaving properly. When he's done, he knows every part and every motion of the engine he's working on. The engine runs smoothly because he has first made all the parts run smoothly.

For example: When you *play* a composition, you start at the beginning and play through until the end. If you stop in the middle, that's a big mistake. But when you *practice*, you take on the mechanic's mindset. You rarely play a composition from beginning to end. Instead, you break the composition down into manageable pieces and play them over and over, making sure everything about them is just right.

When you *play* something, it's because you enjoy it. Your enjoyment comes from the experience of playing it well. When you *practice* something, it's because you need to get better at it. Your enjoyment comes from getting better.

Why does this matter? There's a trap that everyone falls into. They think that if they just sit down and play for an hour or so, they're practicing. But they're not. In fact, they're probably not even playing – they're Fooling Around. There's nothing wrong with Fooling Around, unless you're trying to get better on your instrument. If so, then Practicing is what you want to do. And what makes Practicing Practicing is thinking like a mechanic.

PLAYING	PRACTICING
Focus on Music	Focus on Motion
Pleasure comes from playing well	Pleasure comes from getting better
Whole	Parts
Musical logic	Mechanical logic
"How was I just now?"	"Am I getting better?"
Most decisions have already been made	Making decisions all the time
Feeling	Thinking

THE FOURTH BIG IDEA

You know it when your hands know it.

Two clarinet players are sitting side by side in an empty rehearsal hall. They have their clarinets in hand. On the music stands in front of them are identical copies of the score for Mozart's Clarinet Concerto in A. You need to hire one of them. Pete is on the left; Pat is on the right.

Pete can tell you everything there is to know about the Clarinet Concerto. He knows the starting key, and all the keys he will have to travel through. He knows the form; he understands all the underlying harmonies. He can tell you the date of the first performance; he can even tell you Mozart's birthday (January 27, 1756, at around 10:00 PM.) But – Pete can't actually play the concerto.

Pat, on the other hand, doesn't know anything about Mozart. He knows what key the piece starts it, and he might be able to figure out the rest if you give him enough time and give him a few hints here and there. But - Pat can play the concerto perfectly all the way through.

So who do you hire: Pete or Pat?

MIND AND BODY

The main reason most of us practice is so that we can play music better. Nobody practices so that they can talk about music better, or think about it better. Practicing is primarily about playing, and that means practicing is also about the body.

What about the mind? The mind is important, obviously, and practicing trains the mind as well. But to get the most out of your practicing, you need to put your brain in the back seat and let your hands drive.

Here's why.

The mind and the body learn in different ways. The mind learns by recognizing patterns that connect new information with things it has already learned. So, for example, once a child learns what a dog is, she can recognize that a beagle, a collie and a dachshund are all dogs without anyone telling her – because in her mind she has a pattern for 'dog.' In the same way, a music student who understands the C scale can learn the G scale very quickly, because he can see the patterns that apply to both of them. The mind covers a lot of ground very quickly this way, capturing patterns and filling in the details later.

The body, on the other hand, learns by repetition. For your muscles to learn a motion they have to do it over and over again. There's no capturing patterns and filling in the details later. The hands, especially, need the details *now*, and if you don't pay attention to those details, your hands will learn the wrong ones and it will be very hard to unlearn them.

All that repetition takes time. There aren't any shortcuts. You can't hurry it – in fact, hurrying usually makes you move backwards instead of forwards. And you can't decide in advance how long it should take; it's going to take however long your fingers need it to take. That's just how bodies work.

What does this mean for us? It means that whenever we practice something, *our heads learn it before our hands do.*

Suppose I'm practicing a G scale on my guitar. I run through it slowly two or three times, and my mind says, "OK! Got it! Exactly like the C scale, just moved over a little bit. That was easy - what's next?" My fingers, on the other hand, are having trouble getting from one note to the next, even at this slow speed, and my right shoulder, which my mind doesn't even notice, is hurting because I'm not sitting up straight. My fingers keep working on the scale, but now my mind doesn't have anything to do. It has already figured out the patterns in the G scale and connected them to the C scale it already knows – and it's bored. "Let's do something else!" it says. "Something fun!" And so, faced with a choice between doing something hard (working on the G scale) and something fun (trying something new), I of course choose to do something fun. The G scale, which I have now learned to play badly, has to wait until tomorrow.

It happens all the time. You'll be working on a scale, an exercise or an etude, and at some point you'll say, "Aha! I *understand* it now," and think you're done. But you're not. You aren't done until you say, "Aha! I *can play* it now!"

> *You know it when your hands know it.*

Here's another reason why you need to put your hands in charge.

Let's get back to Pete and Pat. Remember that Pete knows all about the concerto but can't actually play it; Pat doesn't know that much about the concerto, but he can play it perfectly. We can say that Pete has successfully *studied* the concerto, and Pat has successfully *practiced* the concerto. Pete has the concerto in his *head*; Pat has the concerto in his *hands*. Getting the music into the hands is the point of practicing; it's the reason Pat sits down with his clarinet every morning.

By putting your hands in charge, you are keeping your attention focused on what you set out to accomplish. You are making sure you do what you set out to do. It sounds so simple, but it makes all the difference in the world.

HOW DOES THAT HELP?

What does this idea mean for us? How does it help us improve our practicing?

You know it when your hands know it helps us decide what to pay attention to when we practice. We saw earlier that practicing is searching for the ideal movements needed to perform a piece of music. So even though there's a lot more going on when we practice, movement is our primary concern. (Remember The Second Big Idea – *Practice motion. Music will follow.*) The more we focus on making sure our hands know and understand what to do – in other words, the more we concentrate on how our hands have to move – the faster we'll progress.

So: if you want your hands to learn ideal movement, what should you pay attention to when you practice? Your hands.

(Neurologist Dr. Frank Wilson, who has written a lot about both hands and music, points out that there's no reason to think of the hand as something that stops at the wrist. The muscles and tendons that move the fingers reach back to the elbow and the shoulder; the nerves that send signals to the hand attach to the spinal column, and the signals themselves originate in the brain. So, as far as practicing is concerned, everything from your fingertips back through your arm and into your brain counts as your hand.)

To be more specific:

Pay attention to which fingers you use. Write down your fingerings. Question the fingerings printed in the sheet music if they don't feel right, but don't change them until you understand why the editors chose them.

Pay attention your fingertips. With some instruments – guitar, for example – most of your physical contact with the instrument is with your fingertips. Therefore most of what you do – play loud or soft, slow or fast, high or low – you do through your fingertips.

Pay attention to the whole Frank Wilson hand. What are your wrists doing? What are your forearms doing? Where are your elbows? How do your shoulders feel?

Pay attention to physical sensation. How does each motion feel? Notice any pain you're feeling, and change your motions until the pain goes away.

Analyze the sound you make as you play to see what it tells you about what your hands are doing. Are you squeaking on the strings? Figure out what your hands are doing, and change it. Are you hitting two keys at once, or hitting the same wrong key every time? Figure out what your hands are doing, and change it. Are you getting tangled up when you try to play faster or louder? Figure out what your hands are doing, and change it.

You know it when your hands know it.

THE FIFTH BIG IDEA

You affect everything by concentrating on one thing.

Practicing is, in one way, like eating.

You are never just eating; you're eating *something*. And we can be very specific about what that something is. For example: you may say you're eating breakfast, but if we're specific we can say you're really eating corn flakes with milk, sugar and a sliced banana, one spoonful at a time. And if you're paying close attention, you can see, taste, smell or feel each of those things separately – the sweet sugar, the crunchy cereal, the cold milk, and the soft banana.

In the same way, you are never just practicing; you're practicing *something*. For example: you may say you're practicing, but you're really practicing "Stairway to Heaven" or a Chopin nocturne. And if we're specific, we could say you're practicing a certain phrase that's four beats long; we could say you're practicing playing on your fingertips; we could say you're practicing playing as smoothly as possible. The more specific you can be about the thing you're practicing, the better your practicing will be.

But is that specific enough? What else could you be concentrating on? Imagine that you're working on the simplest piece of music you know. How many different things are going on?

- Right hand position
- Right hand motion
- Left hand position
- Left hand motion
- Fingering (is it comfortable? Does it make sense?)
- Tone (is each note sounding clearly?)
- Volume
- Tempo (are you playing at the right speed?)
- Timing (are the notes all the same distance apart?)
- Posture (What are your arms, shoulders, neck, back, legs and feet doing as you play?)
- Breathing
- Are you relaxed? Does any part of your body hurt?
- Are you concentrating?
- etc., etc. etc.

And, of course, you have to play the right notes.

All of these things are interconnected, and they change constantly while you play, sometimes with every note. Each minute there are dozens of these moving targets to hit. Often they are things you're not used to paying attention to, like posture or breathing. Many will never appear in the written music you're trying to play. They're all under your control, and they all need to be right. How do you attend to them all?

Here's the secret: if you concentrate on making one thing better, other things will start to get better, too. Why? Because motion connects everything.

You get better at playing when your motions get better. When you get better, the whole music-driven hands- arms-legs-ears mechanism starts to operate more smoothly and efficiently. Once that happens, it's smooth and efficient for scales; it's smooth and efficient for arpeggios; it's smooth and efficient for *Stairway to Heaven*. That doesn't mean you won't always be making improvements to the mechanism. But the improvements tend to spread throughout the whole system.

This is how you do it.

First of all, we have to separate *concentration* from *thinking*. These are two different things. Thinking tends to be active. You're making decisions, weighing alternatives, trying to understand things. Concentration tends to be reactive: you're noticing what's going on and adjusting to it.

Do as much of your thinking before you start as possible:

- make sure you have whatever tools you need at hand – sheet music, pencil, eraser, metronome, tuner, etc.

- decide which section of music you're going to work on;

- understand as much as you can about what you're about to play

- decide what you're going to concentrate on.

The last one is very important. You can concentrate on any one of those many things that are going on while you play even the simplest music. The more specific you can be, the better.

Watch out for this trap:

"I'm just going to concentrate on getting it right."

If you don't already have it right, *something specific is wrong*. Figure out the specific thing that's wrong and concentrate on that.

Once that's all decided, don't think about it anymore. It's time to start concentrating. As you play, relax and try to notice as much as possible:

- Watch: For most of us, our eyes are much more precise than our ears. They collect a lot more information, too.

- Listen: What does the sound you're making tell you about how you're moving? A weak sound comes from weak motion.

- Feel: Music is not what we do; it's the result of what we do. Motion is what we can control. How does what you're doing feel to your fingers and hands? How do your shoulders feel as you move your hands?

Use your eyes, your ears, your hands, and the rest of your body. Each will have something different for you. Check in with them, one after another, over and over, as you play. If your attention drifts away, gently shift it back.

Keep in mind that there's always more than one thing going on. This means that even when you're concentrating on one thing, you're making progress on others. Concentrate on timing, and your tone will improve. Concentrate on posture, and your breathing will improve. Concentrate on hand position and everything will improve. Why does this work? Because these are all just different ways to approach the same underlying thing: motion.

THE SIXTH BIG IDEA

Don't worry about the hard parts.

People learning a new song or a new technique often get nervous or anxious when they reach "the hard part." 90% of the time the hard part is hard for one (or both) of two reasons:

1.   They're playing it too fast.

2.   They don't understand what they're doing yet.

Here's how you can get rid of 90% of the so-called hard parts:

1.   Slow down.

2.   Cut them into smaller, easier-to-understand pieces and work on those first.

Take the hard parts and slice them up and slow them down until you have parts that are manageable – parts that you can practice without struggling. They can be as small as two notes. Then, when you know them well, put them back together.

Practicing music that's too hard is frustrating and discouraging, and it makes your body tense up. And if you practice frustration, discouragement and tension, you'll start getting better and better at being frustrated, discouraged and tense. You'll end up practicing poor performance – practicing your mistakes until you can make them reliably every time. Better to get a bunch of small pieces perfect first, and then put them all together.

So, if you find yourself struggling, take that as a sign that you need to change your approach. Stop and take a breath; stretch your neck and shoulders. Whatever you're working on, cut it in half – half the notes, half the speed, half the complexity. Think through the material once again. Visualize your hands playing it slowly, smoothly and correctly. Get smaller and go slower and, oddly enough, you'll get where you're going faster.

Once you get used to making progress by getting small and going slow, you'll find that you treat the run-through with great respect. (A run-through is when you play a piece from beginning to end.) If you play a song over and over again – especially if you're playing it badly, as we tend to do when we're learning – you'll get tired of it quickly. The beauty and mystery that give the song life will vanish. You won't enjoy practicing, and by the time you've learned the song you'll be so sick of it you won't want to play it ever again.

Plus, run-throughs are just not an efficient way to get better. Imagine a basketball player trying to improve his foul shooting by playing four quarters of full-court five-on-five. Imagine a golfer working on his putting by playing 18 holes of golf.

So, small and slow and slow is the way to go. Save the run-throughs for when all the 'hard parts' are gone.

THE SEVENTH BIG IDEA

Get your hands and your ears used to "Perfect."

One of the main reasons we practice is to take things we do consciously and make them unconscious. In other words, we think about things in practice so that we can forget about them when we play.

Once we master these things through practice – things like how to finger a note, how to hold or sit at an instrument, how to play louder or softer, how to play a scale or a chord – we want to be able to do them again and again, the same way, without having to think about them.

So: If you were going to decide today how you were going to do something for the rest of your life, wouldn't you want it to be perfect? Or would you say, "Every time I play this piece for the next 50 years, I'm going make some mistakes."

But the truth is, you *are* deciding, every time you practice, how you're going to play for the rest of your life. If you don't aim for "perfect," you'll build "imperfect" into your playing, and it's very hard to undo that.

"Perfect" doesn't mean playing a 5 minute piece perfectly. It means playing a note as perfectly as you can. It means moving your hands from one note to the next as perfectly as you can. It means aiming for perfect tone and perfect timing. It means aiming for perfection note-by-note, instant-by-instant. Forget about playing a whole song perfectly. Put your effort and intention into practicing perfect hand motions, and perfect performances will follow.

Notice that the Seventh Big Idea doesn't say *Play perfectly*. That's a big idea – a little scary, a little vague - that sounds impossible. The Seventh Big Idea says, *Get your hands and your ears used to "Perfect"*. Raise your standards. Get your hands used to moving perfectly, and they won't be satisfied with anything less. Get your ears used to hearing perfect notes and phrases, and anything less than perfect will sound like a mistake. Make perfection at the lowest level a habit. Reach the point where "Good enough" doesn't sound or feel right, where "Good enough" isn't good enough. If you aim for "perfect" every time you practice, your practicing and your playing will both improve.

Don't worry about it being hard. You just need to make one small thing at a time perfect, and do that over and over again, every day. It's the easiest route to perfect playing.

THE FIRST GOOD HABIT

Be comfortable.

It's important to be comfortable while you practice. If you're comfortable, you'll practice longer. If you're comfortable, your body will be relaxed, your breathing will be more natural, and your hands, arms, shoulders, etc. will be freer to move. As a result it will be easier to find the ideal motions you search for as you practice.

Once you're used to being relaxed and comfortable when you practice, you'll begin to notice when you aren't. That will be a sign that you need to make a change. If that happens, stop and figure out what it is. Of course, "comfortable" doesn't mean you can lie down on the coach with your feet up, and "relaxed" doesn't mean "sleepy". "Comfortable" means your body is at ease, free of unnecessary tension and ready to play, and your mind is calm, composed and alert.

It seems so simple and sensible, but it's surprising how frequently we forget. Here are some suggestions.

Use a comfortable chair or piano bench that is the right height. Adjust it until it fits you perfectly. If you're standing, wear comfortable shoes. (And are you sure you have to stand?) If you need a stand or strap for your instrument, spend all the time you need to get it set up exactly right.

Be aware of your posture as you play, especially your neck, shoulders and back. Don't forget your legs and feet, too, especially if you're a pianist, organist or drummer.

If you can, **establish a dedicated practice area** that has good lighting; room for your instrument, notebook and tools; electrical outlets if you need them; a music stand; and a writing surface at the right height. (Remember that a reading surface and a writing surface have different requirements.) It may help you to give this area an identity of its own - a desk, a workbench, a laboratory, a shrine, an oasis, a musical kitchen, a garden, a retreat - whatever works for you. Decorate it; make it comfortable.

Clear your head before you start to practice. Go to the bathroom. Drink a glass of water. If at all possible, put someone else in charge of the phone and the doorbell. (And really – is the phone so important that you can't get away from it for half an hour?)

Shake out your neck, shoulders, arms and hands before you get started. Get up and stretch during your practice sessions. Write it in your notebook (more on that later), "After 15 minutes, stretch for 1 minute."

Of course, you say – doesn't everyone do that? Well —

- Have you ever had to stop practicing because your shoulder hurt, or your eyes were tired, or your back was stiff – even though your shoulder, or your eyes, or your back felt fine before you started to practice?

- Have you ever spent half of your practice time leaning over your instrument so that you could read or write on something on your music stand, instead of setting the instrument aside so you could read and write comfortably?

- Have you ever started to practice and then gotten up after 10 minutes to get your glasses, or a pencil, or a glass of water, or some music?

- Have you ever come up with a way to play something that required difficult finger gymnastics to execute, only to find a much easier way to play it later on?

Be Comfortable.

THE SECOND GOOD HABIT

Be Honest.

Honesty is simple. Ask yourself these questions as you practice:

1. Am I actually doing what I think I'm doing?

2. What am I doing besides what I think I'm doing?

Not easy, but simple.

Notice that the questions aren't about what you're *playing* – they're about what you're *doing*.

Musicians hear music in their heads all the time. When you practice, you have to be careful about this. You have to listen, not to the music in your head, but to *what you actually hear*, and you have to be honest with yourself about it.

- Did I hit that note cleanly, or did I flub it and say, "Close enough"?

- Did I play every note in that fast passage exactly right, or did I get the first few and the last few, with a bunch of mush in the middle?

- Did I play at the right tempo all the way through, or did I speed up in some parts and hesitate or slow down in others? Did I stop when I turned the page?

There are some non-musical sounds to notice, too:

- Is my chair squeaking?

- Am I humming along while I play?

- Am I breathing so loudly that someone could hear it over the music?

When you practice, every sound is your doing – after all, you're the only one there. Wrong notes, weak notes, bad tone, grunts, sighs - whether you mean them or not, they're all yours. You have to control them, and to do that you have to know – and admit – that you're making them.

But wait – there's still more:

- Am I leaning forward and squinting at the music because the music stand is too far away?

- Are my shoulders all bunched up?

- Am I holding my breath?

All of these things are mistakes, which you can't fix without noticing that you've made them.

Music has its own logic, and as musicians we naturally follow and respect that logic. For example, we like to play a whole melody – we don't like to stop in the middle. And we like to play it at a tempo that 'sounds right' – we don't like to play it too slow or too fast.

When we practice, this tendency makes us think that if we follow that musical logic – if we play the melody all the way through, for example – that we must have played it right. But this is like a man driving home from the grocery store and thinking he did it right because he arrived at home – even if he ran a red light, drove over his neighbor's lawn, and left the groceries in the parking lot.

When you practice you can't be distracted by the musical logic. You have to notice what's *really going on*. This is why we think of motion, not music. This is why we go slow. This is why we have to be honest.

There are three mechanical devices that help with Honesty. They don't cover everything, and they need us to ask our two questions in order for them to work, but they help.

1. A <u>metronome</u> provides steady, mechanically accurate pulse. Just like no one automatically knows how to practice, most people don't know automatically how to practice to a metronome. It's not as easy as it looks. There's a chapter on playing with metronomes later in the book.

2. A <u>tuner</u> provides an accurate tone to which you can tune your instrument. This matters most of all to string players. (Igor Stravinsky is supposed to have said, "Harpists spend half their time tuning and the other half playing out of tune.") It's a little less of an issue for players of some other instruments; keyboardists mostly get a free ride here.

3. A <u>recorder</u> is like a mirror, with the same potential for good and for evil. If you can, record some of your practicing and listen to it. It will help you understand what you really sound like. But then, get back to work. Listening to yourself can be helpful, but it's not practicing.

Remember that practicing is different from playing. We're trying to get better. And to get better we have to be honest about where we are. A mechanic who doesn't know what's wrong with an engine, and won't try to find out, can't get it running correctly. He (and we) has to recognize what's wrong in order to fix it.

THE THIRD GOOD HABIT

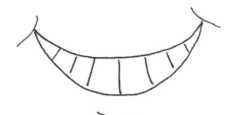

Be Optimistic.

Y ou have at least two good reasons to be optimistic when you practice:

- *Practicing works*, especially when you do it right.

- *Optimism works*. In any enterprise, not just practicing, optimism gives you a clear advantage. Optimists always get farther than pessimists or realists.

When you practice you spend a lot of time working on things you can't do. Most of what you accomplish takes more than one session. Often progress happens over days or weeks; you'll frequently finish your day's practicing thinking that you haven't gotten anywhere.

As an optimist, you look at the list of things you can't do and see every one of them as an accomplishment that just hasn't happened yet. Everything on today's *can't do* list is already on tomorrow's *can do* list – or, if not tomorrow, then the day after that, or the day after that. *Can't do* is temporary; *can do* is long-term. Optimism looks forward to the time when you've already accomplished your goals, and helps pull you toward that time.

You will spend most of your practice time working on things you can't do. But you can change that. Up until now, there have been things you *can do*, and things you *can't do*. From this moment on, there are no things you can't do. There are things you *can do*, and things you *can't do yet*.

Remember that people all over the world, for hundreds of years, have been learning to play musical instruments. They've all gone through the same frustration, and they've all learned to do what you're learning to do. So don't worry. You'll get there.

In an hour of practice you'll make literally thousands of small motions and small decisions. They'll add up to an inch of progress on a good day. The process is slow; it requires patience. But it's real.

Start each practice session with the belief that you're going to make progress. Throughout the session, notice the progress you make and appreciate it. Write it down. Remember that your steps forward will, on a daily basis, be small. That's the nature of practicing. Come back again and again to the idea that you can do what you're setting out to do. If you get frustrated or discouraged, remember that that's part of the process. Make optimism permanent, and frustration and discouragement will always be temporary.

Have faith in tomorrow. Trust the process. End each session with optimism, even if you worked hard and didn't end up where you wanted to be. One of these tomorrows will turn out to be the today you get there.

THE FOURTH GOOD HABIT

Be Persistent.

Practicing requires that we do some things that don't come naturally, and that we don't do some things that do come naturally. It's natural to do things that are easy, and not to do things that are hard. It's natural to play things we already know, instead of things we don't know. It's natural to stop doing things that frustrate us.

When you're practicing, and you're dealing with something that seems hard to do, the easiest thing in the world is to give up. That's what most people do. Either they stop practicing completely, or they stop working on the things they can't do yet and just play the things they already know. Sometimes they just go through the motions, stumbling through a piece or an exercise over and over without concentrating on it. That's not practicing – that's fooling around. And it's not even *good* fooling around, because it's a lousy way to spend your time. *If you're not enjoying it, change it until you do.*

People who lift weights know that the real progress happens when they keep going after their bodies and minds tell them to stop. When you practice, you have to do the same. You have to be persistent.

Persistence is partly just making a plan for your practice session and sticking with it. But it's more than just that. If you decide you're going to practice an etude for 15 minutes, you don't stop at 11 minutes. You complete the tasks you set for yourself. But if you're bored at 11 minutes, don't stop, and don't just soldier on, either – first, get un-bored. Find a way to make it interesting. If it's too hard, don't stop, don't soldier on – find a way to make it simpler, and continue practicing. That's persistence in a nut shell:

Find a way, and continue.

The First Big Idea says: If you don't enjoy practicing, change it until you do. Are you bored? Then you're not enjoying practicing. Don't give up, and don't just keep at it; change something. Focus your attention, and you won't be bored. Make it enjoyable, then keep at it. Do the same if you're frustrated, or puzzled, or lost. Change something. Make it enjoyable, then keep at it.

Persistence is not just applying relentless effort. Persistence is arming yourself with intelligence, optimism, imagination, curiosity, a sense of humor and all of your *First, Learn to Practice* ideas, habits and tools, and *then* applying relentless effort.

Picture a man beating his head on a wall. On the ground behind him are a sledgehammer, a ladder tall enough to get him over the wall and a key to the door in the wall. And yet he's still banging his head. Is that being persistent?

Persistence is not plowing bravely through obstacles; it's smartly removing the obstacles so you can get back to work.

Here's the key to persistence in practical terms. Make a plan for your practice session and do everything in the plan. If you can look back at the session with pride and look forward to the next one with optimism, you've been persistent.

THE FIFTH GOOD HABIT

Be Consistent.

I magine planning to climb a mountain this way:

> *"I'm going to climb on Friday. Then I'm going to Nantucket for the weekend, and I'll be tired on Monday, so I'll try to pick up where I left off on Tuesday and climb a little more. Wednesday might be good, I'm not sure, but Thursday I'll definitely try to climb again, and I know I can probably find some time on the weekend."*

How far up the mountain would that get you?

Practice works best when you do it every day. Some people would say that's pretty much the only way it works. Being consistent means practicing the right way, every day. Being consistent means being persistent every day.

(Of course, life happens; it's hard to practice every day. We're aiming for 'perfect' even if we don't always get there.)

When you practice you're building mental and physical habits. You're developing concentration by training your mind to work in certain ways. You're developing stamina by training your muscles to do things they don't normally do. You're trying to learn things so thoroughly that you can do them without thinking.

Many of the things you're trying to learn are small movements that are hard to describe in words. ("It sounds better when my fingers go like *this* instead of like *that*.") In order to be able to repeat these movements, you have to be able to remember how your hands feel or look when you make them. You can't really write them down, and that makes them hard to remember. If you let a few days elapse between practice sessions, you'll forget them, and you'll have to find them all over again. It will be as though your last practice session never happened.

Being consistent means you have a plan, you stick to it, and you do it every day. Practicing every day is much more important than practicing for a particular amount of time. 20 minutes a day works better than 60 minutes every three days. Consistency makes all the difference. It's the best way to get there.

If you practice a little here and a little there – if you practice scales on one day, and songs on another day, and fiddle around with your instrument while you watch tv on another day – if your practicing is inconsistent and disconnected – you'll be starting at the bottom of the mountain every time you take up your instrument.

Consistency works for another reason. You can't be consistent without commitment. You can't make a practice plan, and a schedule, and stick to it for any length of time, without making some kind of promise to yourself. Being consistent means you have jumped in with both feet. It means you have told yourself, "I want to be a musician, and if this is what it takes then I'm going to do it. No excuses, no distractions." That's a powerful promise.

THE SIXTH GOOD HABIT

Go slow.

Ilf there were going to be a book about practicing that couldn't be more than two words long, it would be this: *GO SLOW.*

Here's why.

<u>Practicing slowly</u> gives you the time and space to focus on the details of each note you play and each movement you make. When you play at quicker tempos, things go by too fast. If you play eighth notes at 60 beats per minute, each note will take half a second. How much can you tell about any one note before the next one comes along? If you play nothing but eighth notes for two minutes, you'll play 240 notes. How much can you remember, after all those notes, about how well you played any one of them?

<u>Practicing slowly</u> makes it easier for you to focus on the mechanics – that is, on what your hands, arms, shoulders, breath, etc. are doing. This is because the slower you go, the less what you're working on sounds like music. The less it

sounds like music, the easier it is to ignore. And if you're going to concentrate on the motion, you have to ignore the music.

Music has logic that all musicians find compelling. We like to play things from beginning to end. We like to hear complete melodies. But that's not what practicing is about. Remember Big Idea #2: *Practice Motion. Music will follow.* We have to set aside the musical logic and follow the mechanical logic.

<u>Practicing slowly</u> encourages relaxation in your hands and arms. Practicing fast does the opposite. You learn and perfect the motions slowly, with tension-free muscles. Later, when you speed the motions up, your muscles have learned to play without tension, so they stay relaxed even at performance speeds.

<u>Practicing slowly</u> makes it possible to answer the two questions from the Second Good Habit, *Be Honest*:

1. Am I actually doing what I think I'm doing?

2. What am I doing besides what I think I'm doing?

When you go slow, you can answer those questions; when you go fast, you can't. There's just too much going on – too many things happening at once.

<u>Practicing slowly</u> makes mistakes impossible to overlook. If you make a mistake playing at 300 notes per minute, you may not even notice you've made it; if you do notice it, you'll probably forget it by the end of the song. And you certainly don't have time to figure out what went wrong, and then fix it, at that speed. If you make the same mistake while you're playing 30 notes per minute, you'll catch it, and you'll be able to fix it.

How slow should you go?

- Slow enough to play perfectly.

- Slow enough to hear the spaces between the notes.

- Slow enough to see all, hear all, feel all, and know all.

THE SEVENTH GOOD HABIT

Make music.

W̲e know that playing and practicing are two different things. But what we're playing or practicing is always music. Scales, arpeggios, exercises, obscure little 200-year-old pieces by composers we're never heard of – all music.

It's easy to forget that when we're practicing. We're searching for ideal motion, after all. We execute movements over and over to find just the right way to do them. We repeat melodic fragments dozens of times in order to build muscle memories. We play combinations of notes that we've put together solely for the mechanical effort it takes to play them, not for their musical effect. Can we really play this –

Repeat 1,000 times:

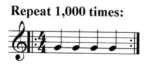

- and intend it to sound like music?

Yes.

The muscles in your hands have no taste. They can't learn and remember a 'practice' way of playing and then, later on when you've got an audience, dig down deep and find a 'performance' way of playing. 99 times out of 100, your muscles will do what you have <u>taught</u> them to do, not what you <u>command</u> them to do.

If you practice with a clanky, mechanical sound, you will build that sound into your hands. If you practice with a dogged, let's-get-it-over-with attitude, you'll build that attitude into your posture and your playing. You will create bad habits that you'll never unlearn.

On the other hand, if you regard everything you practice as music, the little changes in motion that turn scales into melodies will become habits. Most of those changes will be so subtle that you can only produce them by thinking "Make this musical." There's no other way to get at them.

If you move musicality into your hands it will become automatic, and they will be incapable of clankiness.

Making music is different from *following the logic of the music.* We've talked about that elsewhere – adopting the mechanic's mindset, emphasizing motion over music, going slow, etc. *Make Music* means to build a musical intention, a musical attitude, a musical effect, into every note, every rest, every finger movement, every breath. When you hit that target, you'll be unable to play any other way. You want musicality to be something automatic, requiring no thought. The only way to get there is note by note, every time.

This idea may not make sense at first; the process is hard to describe with words. (Music is full of ideas like that.) You may ask, "How do I do that?" The answer – "Just keep the idea in mind, and sooner or later you'll see it start to happen" – isn't all that satisfying. But that's how you do it.

TOOLS

The Metronome

For many of us, the first time we turn on a metronome is when a music teacher says, "Practice this piece with a metronome." But how, exactly, do you do that? No one is born knowing about metronomes, so, before you can get much out of them, you have to learn how to use them.

What is it?

A metronome is like a very precise but very dull drummer. It produces a steady stream of clicks at any speed you like, usually from 40 beats per minute to 200 beats per minute. Your task is to play at the same speed, lining up the notes you play with the clicks of the metronome.

Why use a metronome?

A metronome helps you train yourself to play in time. Playing in time means giving each note and each rest the right value, and doing that consistently throughout a piece of music.

Playing in time is something you do *unconsciously*. It is much more physical than mental. The body, not the mind, is in charge. You play in time when your ears, your hands and your heartbeat get synced up; your mind tends to just get in the way. You can't really think your way into playing in time; you have to feel it. Training with a metronome brings this unconscious process closer to the surface so we can work on it.

How do you train with a metronome?

Several things have to happen, all at the same time, for you to play along with a metronome. You have to listen to the metronome and sense when it is going to make its next 'click.' Your hands have to be able to play your note *exactly* when you intend to. You have to be able to tell whether you played your note on time, and adjust accordingly for the next note. And you have to do this over and over again, in real time, without stopping, and without thinking. That's a lot happening at once, so, when you're learning how to do it, it's good to make things as simple as possible.

Here are the fundamentals of working with a metronome.

1. Relax your body.

2. Quiet your mind.

3. Listen, and keep listening.

4. Play, and keep playing.

The fundamentals stay the same regardless of the music you're working on.

Learning how

You can learn how to use a metronome one minute at a time. Try this:

1. Take up your instrument; relax your body and quiet your mind.

2.   Turn on the metronome and set it at 60 beats per minute (1 beat per second.)

3.   Listen for five or ten seconds. Let your body get used to the pulse so that you can feel when each click is coming. If your body starts moving in time with the click, that's good.

4.   Pick a single note and play it at the same time (but not as loud) as each metronome click. Listen to the clicks and the notes. Don't think about whether your notes are early, late or on time; just listen and play. Stay relaxed; keep your mind quiet; keep listening; and keep playing. You will naturally sync up with the metronome.

5.   Stop after one minute; shut the metronome off, stretch a little and then start again.

Remember: it's physical, not mental. The reason for relaxing the mind, and listening for ten seconds first, and not trying, is to put the body in charge. The mind gets bored with repetitive activity like this very quickly. It looks for things that change; it craves novelty and hates repetition. But the body needs repetition in order to learn, and the metronome is for training the body. That's why we have to quiet the mind.

Once the body is in charge, syncing up happens naturally. Bodies like rhythm, and they like syncing to it. That's why you unconsciously tap your foot to music you like. You don't think about it; in fact, it usually happens when you're *not* thinking about it. So you don't have to worry about getting in sync with the metronome. Just relax and let it happen. If you stick to the fundamentals, it doesn't take too long to get the hang of it.

This one-minute exercise is like a push-up. No one ever got strong doing one push-up a day, but if you put a bunch of them together every day for a few weeks, you'll get results. After you've done it for a while, you will be able to set the speed higher, play longer, and still sync up easily and consistently. At that point, you've learned how to use a metronome.

There are two important things to know that seem so incredibly obvious that they're not worth mentioning. Maybe that's why NOBODY EVER SEEMS TO REMEMBER THEM.

You have to be able to hear the metronome. You may have to play softer than usual, but that's OK. The metronome should be the thing you're most aware of. It can't do its job in the background.

The metronome will not adjust to you. You have to adjust to the metronome. This is one reason we say "keep listening." It's easy to start off listening to the metronome and end up ignoring it and listening instead to the music we're playing. That's just like not turning it on in the first place.

Some tips

1. *Think before you start.* If you have to think about what you're doing while you train with the metronome, your mind won't be quiet, and your body won't be in charge. So, before you start, learn the music you're going to play well enough that you don't have to struggle with it. Figure out the notes and the timing. Work out all the fingerings, and write them down if you have to. Decide exactly which section of the piece, scale or exercise you're going to train with. (See tip #2.) Understand as much as you can before you start.

2. *Simple music in short segments.* Simple music requires less thinking than complex music, so it's easier to keep your mind quiet and let your body do its work. Short segments allow you to make a lot of repetitions in a short time, which helps your body learn. The worst thing you can do is play the whole song through, over and over again.

3. ***Don't try; just listen.*** If you keep your mind quiet, your body will sooner or later sync up with the metronome by itself. If you try, or if you think too much about being early or late, your mind won't be quiet, and your body won't sync up. Listen, and keep listening; play, and keep playing.

4. ***Be patient.*** Good time takes time. Good time is a physical skill. It comes from moving your muscles a certain way, consistently, for a long time, until they do it automatically. You can't rush it; you can only stick with it.

TOOLS

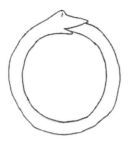

Looping

Practicing involves a lot of repetition. But there's a very specific kind of repetition that makes all the difference. It's not just doing something over and over – it's *Looping*.

Looping means practicing a short section of music over and over, with a specific task in mind, and paying close attention to everything that happens.

Three things make the difference between repetition and looping:

- what you loop

- how you loop it

- noticing

What you loop:

The passage you choose to loop will be a short section cut out of a complete piece of music. It should be short enough to play from memory. It should contain something specific you want to work on, and nothing else. It should be not-too-easy and not-too-hard. If the passage is too easy, it will be boring to practice; if it's too hard, it'll be frustrating to practice.

(This is a good time to point out that what you call "easy" and what you call "hard" depend a lot on what you call "right." The Seventh Big Idea says, "Get your hands and your ears used to 'perfect'". Does that change what you mean by "easy"?)

When you're deciding how to cut your looping passage, make your choice based on motion first, then music. Where are your fingers getting hung up? Where do you hesitate? It may feel natural to work on a whole phrase, because it makes sense musically. But when you're looping, the music is beside the point – in fact, it's a distraction. Motion first.

How you loop it:

Remember the Seventh Big Idea: _Get your hands and your ears used to 'perfect'_. Then start to play your loop over and over slowly, at a speed which allows you to play musically and perfectly.

When you make a mistake – _any_ mistake:

- _Slow down._

- _Correct the mistake right away. If you can, find and correct the cause of the mistake as well._

- _Continue at the new, slower speed._

There are three important ideas here, and they're worth looping through. The first is _Correct the mistake right away_. The second is _Find and correct the **cause** of the mistake_. The third is _Slow down_.

Correct the mistake right away. Don't save anything for later; more often than not, if you don't stop and fix it immediately, you won't even remember it, much less fix it.

*Find and correct the **cause** of the mistake.* It's one thing to realize you played G instead of G#. But *why* did you play G instead of G#? Did you misread the music? Did you not stretch your finger far enough? Did you forget the key signature? Did you get this passage confused with another passage? Did you lose your concentration and start thinking about what you're going to have for lunch? Did your finger just not know where to go? Going back and playing the G# is not enough. You have to know why, and fix that, too.

Slow down. Now we're getting to the heart of things. This is the idea that everyone has heard, and everyone knows is right, and almost nobody is willing to do:

> *Slow things down to a speed at which you can play perfectly and musically. This may be excruciatingly slow, but that's OK.*

The most common mistake most people make when they practice is to try to play everything all the way through, at performance speed, every time. Their goal is not to play a song perfectly; it's to get through it from beginning to end. They set their minds on getting to the end of the piece, and that becomes more important to them than playing it perfectly. They get caught up in the rhythm and the speed and the musical logic of what they're playing; the music says, "You have to finish", and as a result Playing It All beats Playing It Right. They make music the point, and they get trapped by its momentum.

But we're <u>practicing</u>. Music is not the point; *motion* is the point. Music comes later. We're searching for ideal motion. We're paying attention to what we're doing so that we can be sure it's right and so we can change it if we want to. You just can't do that at high speed.

Practicing slowly prevents momentum from taking over. It allows us to focus on the logic of motion instead of the logic of the music. It gives us the time to notice and deal with things that otherwise would go by too fast.

Noticing:

Noticing is a relaxed form of concentration. Most people think of concentration as something that's both tense and intense. Picture a cat stalking a small bird – that's how most people see concentration. Picture a dog lying by your feet, who seems to be asleep but is instantly alert when anything happens – that's noticing.

When we're looping we're catching and fixing mistakes – anything that's not perfect. But we're also keeping ourselves open to spotting small and subtle things that wouldn't seem like mistakes if we weren't aiming for 'perfect'. Things like: Is my body relaxed? Am I producing good tone? Are my fingers moving smoothly? Am I using the right part of my fingertips? Am I focused on what I wanted to focus on when I started the loop? Am I breathing naturally?

And, of course, once you notice something, you make any adjustments you need to make. If your shoulder is tense, relax it. If you're rushing, slow down. If your fingering seems awkward, change it.

Now let's loop through again, and see what else we can notice.

What you loop:

When you're deciding what passage of music to loop, you usually start with a piece of music and cut out a section to focus on. There are three basic ways to cut:

(1)   Vertically: isolate a passage that's at most a few seconds long:

(2) *Horizontally*: cut the treble from bass, the right hand from left hand, the melody from the accompaniment, etc.

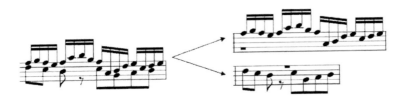

(3) *"Off with their heads!"*: separate the pitch from rhythm

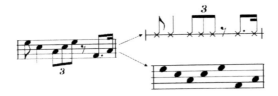

(It's impossible to practice rhythm if you're struggling with motion. As soon as you hesitate for any reason, your rhythm goes out the window. You may know what you should play, but you can't actually play it. If you set aside the pitch, and tap out the rhythm on the table top or play it on a single note, you can master the rhythm first.)

Of course, you can use all three cuts at the same time to get the looping passage down to a manageable size and shape.

Trying to practice a piece by playing the whole thing over and over again – looping without cutting - is a mistake that everybody makes. There are lots of reasons why not to do it. Here are four.

Reason #1: It doesn't work.

Imagine you're working on a piece that's two minutes long and has one hard part that's two seconds long. If you practice it by playing the whole piece over and over, you'll get through it five times in 10 minutes, and you will have played the hard part five times for a total of 10 seconds.

Now imagine that you cut out that hard part, slow it down to half speed, and loop it for 10 minutes. This way you're playing the hard part – the only part you really need to work on – 150 times, and giving it your complete attention for 10 full minutes. That's how to make things perfect.

(Keep in mind that perfect only counts if you can do it every time, on purpose. Perfect by accident isn't perfect – it's accidental.)

Reason #2: It ruins the piece for you.

Looping a whole piece usually means playing it badly. You speed up through the easy parts and slow down or stop in the hard parts. It sounds terrible. Soon your ears (and your hands) get used to hearing 'terrible' instead of 'perfect', and we don't want that.

Clanking through a piece you don't know also saps the beauty and mystery out of it. You don't want to get tired of it before you know how to play it.

Reason #3: It feels like playing instead of practicing.

Remember the Third Big Idea: Playing and Practicing are two different things. They are, in fact, two completely different ways of approaching music.

When you play, you're creating (or recreating) a work of art, and you bring an artist's frame of mind to it. You're trying to create a thing of beauty from a group of notes that mean little or nothing individually. You're looking at the big picture.

When you practice, you're searching for the ideal motions necessary to play a piece of music. You're looking at details. You're examining notes, fingerings, hand movements, etc. and finding the best way to execute them. You bring a mechanic's frame of mind, rather than an artist's.

Trying to practice by playing is like trying to change a tire while you're driving your car.

Reason #4: It makes you struggle.

Every piece starts out with some sections that seem hard and some that don't. If you try to practice by looping the whole piece, you'll never spend enough time on the hard parts to get them under control and make them easy. You'll be fighting the music the whole time.

Remember the Sixth Big Idea - Don't worry about the hard parts – where we said that, as long as you're working on music that's not way beyond your current playing ability, a musical passage that's hard to practice is usually hard because:

1. *You're playing it too fast.   OR*

2. *You don't understand it yet.*

(Occasionally you'll find another explanation, but these are the two main problems.)

Both of these can be fixed by looping the passage that's giving you trouble. Neither one can be fixed by playing the whole piece over and over again.

If you're playing too fast: Slow down until you can play it perfectly and musically, even if it's excruciatingly slow.

If you don't understand it: Cut it into pieces that you can understand, even if there are only two or three notes in each piece; loop the pieces until you understand them; then put them back together.

How you loop it:

Because of the slow speed, the sharp focus and the small amount of material you're working with, looping lets you examine each event within the loop – note, rest, chord, finger movement, hand shift - almost as though someone else is doing it. Picture a mechanic letting an engine run for a long time, just watching it until he understands exactly how it works. That's what looping allows you to do.

The mechanic's frame of mind is essential to good practicing. In fact, if you're sitting at your instrument and you're not in that state of mind, you're probably not practicing. You may be playing, or you may be fooling around, but you're not practicing.

But remember the Fourth Big Idea: You don't know it until your hands know it.

Noticing:

There's always more than one thing going on at a time.

Noticing is Awareness. It has a meditative aspect to it. You are being aware of all the sounds you're making, all the movements you're making and the feelings in your body – in short, everything that's going on. The thoughts in your head, on the other hand, are actually a distraction. Let them fade away as gently as you can. When you're noticing, not thinking is better than thinking.

That completes our second loop through looping.

Looping helps you find the ideal motions for notes, scales, chords, phrases and short passages. It helps you find how your body relates to your instrument in a relaxed and comfortable way. It gives you lots of good, strong parts, but they're like nuts and bolts and springs and levers – they don't do much by themselves. You need to put those parts together into something bigger in order to have what you want. We'll get to that in the next chapter.

TOOLS

MONDAY 9/1 – 1 HOUR
PRACTICE SCALES AND ARPEGGIOS – KEEP THE RIGHT SHOULDER RELAXED!
PRACTICE 1ST SECTION OF 'ELITE SYNCOPATIONS'. REASON: TO MASTER THE
BASS AND TREBLE PARTS SEPARATELY
PLAY 'MOONLIGHT IN VERMONT'. REASON: TO BRING IT BACK TO MIND,
BECAUSE I KNOW AUNT MARIE'S GOING TO ASK ME TO PLAY IT WHEN
SHE VISITS NEXT WEEK
GET UP AND STRETCH FOR A MINUTE
FOOL AROUND WITH 'I'LL BE HOME FOR CHRISTMAS'. REASON: TO SEE IF I
WANT TO LEARN IT FOR THE CHRISTMAS PARTY.
MAKE NOTES FOR TOMORROW.

The Plan

To get the most out of the time you spend practicing – however much time you decide to spend - you need a plan. A plan describes what you are going to do during each practice session. A good one:

- is written down;

- has a list of tasks that are based on goals you set for yourself;

- is relatively constant from day to day.

(If you're studying with a teacher, he or she may help you with your plan. On the other hand, your teacher may say, "Work on these two scales and these three pieces." That's a list of assignments, not a plan.)

The plan is an easy way to build discipline into your routine. Writing it down in advance gives you time to think about it before you start practicing. It helps put you in the mechanic's frame of mind. This will make it easier to stay focused during the practice session. By making decisions in advance about what to work on, you give yourself one less thing to think about; that makes concentration easier.

GOALS

Goals describe why you're practicing. They can be about technique, or songs, or ideas, or styles of music. The best goals are positive, specific and measureable, with target dates and starting points. It's good to have one or two that are a little scary, but also achievable. Here are some samples:

> "By next Thursday I will play an F major scale up and down two octaves, using the correct fingering, without hesitating, without music, in time with the metronome set at 72. Right now I can get through it slowly if I have the music and the fingering in front of me."

> "By January 30 I will perform the Chopin Nocturne Opus 9 Number 1 for my family, from memory, correctly, without hesitation. Today, May 30, I have listened to recordings of the Nocturne and have the sheet music, but have not started to learn it."

> "By February 28 next year, I will participate in a bluegrass jam, playing chords, melodies and solos and singing harmony. Right now, on March 15, I can play chords on most bluegrass songs but I'm nervous about soloing and singing in public."

> "By July 4 I will have worked through the book *Intermediate Music Theory* and will have a firm understanding of everything in it. Today, August 1, I own the book but haven't opened it yet."

Keep your target dates less than a year away to start with. Goals that are too long-term can become pipe dreams if you let them. If it seems like it will take two years to accomplish a goal, break it down into two smaller ones. You may be underestimating (or overestimating) the amount of work it will take to accomplish it. You may not know enough about your goal yet to figure out how to achieve it. And be optimistic – once you've written down your goal, you've taken the first step towards achieving it.

It may help to set up milestones on the way to your goal. If your goal is to play 500 notes per minute, and you're starting at 100 notes per minute, plan to celebrate a bit when you get to 300 notes per minute.

It's important to write your goals down. This keeps them from changing from day to day. Mine are on a 3 x 5 card. The small size of the card forces me to be concise when describing them; it also keeps me from having more goals than I can manage. I use the goals card as a bookmark in my notebook (more on that later), so my goals are always in front of me when I practice.

TASKS

Obviously these goals are way too big to achieve in a single practice session. Instead, we work on them one small piece at a time. Ideally (and we're searching for the ideal) each task we set for a practice session will lead us toward one or more of our goals.

Think of your session plan as a to-do list. Each item on the list is a Task, and each Task has three parts: a Verb, a Noun, and an Idea.

Verbs are the action you're going to take, and, for our purposes, there are not as many as you might think. Here are the big ones:

- Practice

- Learn

- Play

- Fool Around

- Write

- Explore

- Polish

Nouns are things like songs, passages from songs, scales, exercises, techniques and chord progressions.

The **Idea** is the "one thing" from the Fifth Big Idea (*You affect everything by working on one thing.*) It can be the reason you're doing the task, or it can be something to keep in mind while you do it.

Reasons might be:

- to find or refine the right motion;

- to get comfortable with the right motion once you've found it;

- to understand a hard passage and make it less hard;

- to memorize a passage, or

- to build muscle memory of the passage into the hands.

Things to keep in mind might be:

- Keep your fingers curved

- Use your index finger for the G in the first measure

- Stay on the tips of your fingers

- Go slow

Here are some sample tasks:

- "Learn the F harmonic minor scale to understand the notes and fingering."

- "Play Minuet in G to put together all the sections I learned separately."

- "Practice the bass line of measures 9 – 10 of Etude #1 to master the timing before I put the bass and treble parts together."

If you can connect your reasons to a specific goal, so much the better. Life isn't always neat and orderly enough to make this possible; learning the F minor scale may not fit into any goal except getting smarter about music, and that one is a little vague. On the other hand, if one of your goals is to be able to play at 500 notes per minute, any conscientious scale work will help you get there.

You can use all the verbs in your session plan, or you can use one, two or three of them – as long as "Practice" is always one of them. Practice is what makes you a better player. And if you find you're using more than four, you may want to consider sharpening your focus; you may be trying to do too much.

Before we move on, there's one more task to remember that doesn't fit the rules: Get up and stretch for a minute. It's a good one to slip in a few times every session.

TIME

How long is a practice session? That depends on you. It should be long enough that you can get completely into it, and short enough that you finish refreshed and enlivened, not tired and stiff. An hour a day works for some people; half an hour a day works for some people. Half an hour in the morning and another half an hour in the evening works for other people.

The key is concentration. Practice as long as you can concentrate, and not longer. Practicing without concentrating is worse than a waste of time, since it can actually move you backwards, away from your goals.

Twenty minutes of concentrated practicing is better than sixty minutes of unfocused practicing. And it doesn't have to be twenty solid minutes. You can focus on a task for five minutes, then take a break for a minute, and start over again. Your twenty minutes can be four bursts of concentration, each five minutes long, with rests in between. Over time, your ability to concentrate will improve; your bursts will get longer, and you'll be able to string more of them together.

The length of time you practice is connected to the number of tasks you set for yourself. If you try to work on too many things, your attention will be splintered and you won't give any one thing enough time. If you work on too few, you'll get bored.

How much time should you spend on a specific task? The easy but vague answer is "Until you're satisfied." When you feel that you've accomplished something, and that you've done as much on that task as you can for this session, then move on to the next one. Again, concentration is key. If you lose your focus while you're working on a task, take a short break to clear your head. Stretch, get a glass of water, look at the horizon, then get back to practicing. It doesn't matter whether you take up the old task or start a new one, as long as you've renewed your concentration.

This is not how most of us allot our practice time. We say, "Play this scale 5 times" or "Play this piece for 10 minutes." This type of scheduling leaves us saying, "Well, I'm glad that's over with" a lot. We finish each task with a feeling of relief.

But how much better would it be if we finished each task with a feeling of accomplishment? How much better if accomplishing something on every task became a habit?

Once you get into this habit, you'll find that you have to think about cutting short your tasks in order to fit them all in; otherwise a single task can suddenly fill up the whole session.

Until you get there, use a kitchen timer instead of a clock when you're working on tasks for five or ten minutes at the time. With the clock, you have to look up every few minutes and say, "Is it time yet? Am I done?" With the timer, you can concentrate on the task and forget about the time until the timer goes off.

(This is a good time to remember that most people underestimate the amount of repetition necessary to get better at playing an instrument. Earl Scruggs, in his wonderful banjo instruction book, gave one-measure exercises and said, "Play 1,000 times." He wasn't kidding.)

WHAT TO WORK ON

The length of time you practice and the amount of time you spend on each task will affect the number of things you can work on in one session. If you're taking lessons, your teacher will probably assign you certain exercises, pieces and techniques to work on each week. In that case, it may be enough to spend roughly the same amount of time on each assignment. In other words, if you have six things to work on from your teacher, and an hour to practice, then you could spend ten minutes on each one. If you're flexible – that is, if you spend a little more time on the harder tasks and a little less on the easier ones, and add a little time at the end to Play songs you like or to Fool Around a while – that approach could work.

If you're not working with a teacher, you have to set your own practice agenda. Again, this will be tied to your goals, and, again, one size does not fit all. It's helpful to think in terms of a few Big Topics to be working on – things like:

- Technique

- Music Theory

- Learning new repertoire

- Maintaining the repertoire of material you've already learned

- Composing / Arranging

- Preparing for a performance

- Improvisation

- Sight-reading

Unless you are practicing for several hours a day, you won't be able to devote a significant amount of time to each of these topics – so pick three or four, and organize your practice around them:

- *"I'm going to practice for an hour every day. Each day I'll spend 10 minutes on technique, 10 minutes on music theory, 20 minutes on improvisation and 20 minutes on learning new repertoire."*

- *"I'm going to practice for 20 minutes in the morning and 20 minutes at night. I'll spend the morning on technique and theory and the evening on repertoire."*

That gives you a framework for your practicing that will be consistent from day to day. Make sure it works with your goals and tasks, and then stick with it for a few months. Adjust it if you need to, but aim for a routine that doesn't change once you've settled on it.

To keep yourself on track from week to week, you may find it helpful to line up your practice session plans. Before you write today's session plan, look at yesterday's plan and the day before yesterday's plan – or, even better, before you write Monday's plan, look at last Monday's plan and Monday-two-weeks-ago's plan. Make sure you're moving towards your goals.

LEARNING VS. PRACTICING

The verbs you'll use most in your tasks are *Learn* and *Practice*. Let's talk a little bit about why we separate these two things that seem to be connected.

Practice is mostly about the hands. We look for ideal motion. We build muscle memory. We push information into our fingers. We aim to be able to play unconsciously, without thinking. We approach what we do with a mechanic's eye, asking "What would make this physical process go more smoothly and efficiently?" We measure our success by *what we can do*, not by *what we can remember*.

Learning is mostly about the head. It means increasing what we understand. It involves getting information out of books; it also involves making connections and drawing conclusions from things we notice while we practice.

Learning and Practicing are often happening at the same time. In fact, if you're serious about Learning or serious about Practicing, you can't really do one without the other. You can't Learn without Practicing; you can't Practice without Learning.

So: Why do we separate them?

Because practicing is what moves you toward your goals.

Playing music is a physical act. It's a sport for your fingers. They have to be able to move with strength, speed, grace and precision. The only way to get them there is through extraordinary physical activity. Without the hands, what you learn is not music – it's music theory. It's necessary and important, but, without practicing, it doesn't make you a better player.

Separating practicing from learning helps us focus on one thing: how our hands move, in detail. That focus is how we will find strength, speed, stamina, grace and precision. It's how we move from *can't* to *can*. That focus turns ordinary physical activity into extraordinary physical activity. We separate practice, and lean heavily on it, to make that focus happen.

Because learning and practicing require different mindsets.

It might be even clearer to say that Learning and Practicing *are* different mindsets. When we Learn we take in information from outside and move it inside. When we Practice we observe motion through sight, sound and touch and try to analyze, understand and improve it. Learning music involves words, ideas, numbers and symbols. Practicing music involves motion, touch and the feelings in our muscles. Learning music has no 'real time' component; in Practicing, time is essential. Learning doesn't have to involve motion; Practicing doesn't exist without it. Learning requires thinking; Practicing requires moving. Learning has an external focus; Practicing is more internal. Practicing has a meditative aspect that Learning does not have.

Our minds operate one way when we Practice, and another way when we Learn. Better to take advantage of that than to fight it.

We talk most about Practicing here, but Learning is not less important than Practicing; it's just separate.

LEARNING AND PRACTICING, PART 2

So, with all that being said, how do I decide, when I'm writing down the tasks in my practice session plan, what's learning and what's practicing?

The easiest way to decide is this. If paper is involved, you're mostly learning. If it's just you and your instrument, you're mostly practicing.

The only reason to work with paper – sheet music, theory books, tablature, etc. – is that the information on the paper is not in your head. Learning means getting it off the paper and into your head. This may require to you use your instrument, of course, and while you're learning, you can't really focus on your hands and what they're doing. So that's learning, not practicing. Once the information is in your head, the only useful thing to do with it is to transfer it to your hands. You do that by practicing.

Try this approach: open the book, memorize a short passage, close the book, and practice the passage. Working this way helps separate the inquisitive learning mindset from the meditative practice mindset. It also separates two *physical* states:

- *Learning*, which usually involves you, your instrument, a book, a pencil, reading, writing and head-scratching; and

- *Practicing*, which is just you and your instrument.

In the first one you're leaning over your instrument or holding it on your lap or, if you've been paying attention, putting it on a stand, then picking it up, then putting it down, then picking it up. It's hard to get comfortable like that.

In the second one, you're comfortable, playing your instrument, searching for ideal motion, which by definition includes ideal posture. It's very hard to do that if you're referring back to the book as you play.

WRITING IT ALL DOWN: THE NOTEBOOK

If you have a teacher, he or she may write down your assignments in an assignment book, so you know what to work on every day.

The Notebook is something different. This is *your* book. Your notebook is where you write down your daily practice session plans, plus anything you discover while you practice. It's the rolling documentation of whether you've got your head on straight.

Like session plans, notebooks are like shoes. We all need shoes, but we don't all need the same style or size shoes. Likewise, we all need a notebook, but we all don't need need the same notebook. What fits me may or may not fit you. As long as you're writing things down, whatever format works for you is the right one.

Here's what I do. I use an inexpensive composition book with a cardboard cover, like I used in grammar school. Starting from the front, I write in the session plan for each day's practice before I start. If I need to write anything down while I'm learning, I do it right under the practice plan. When I make discoveries – things I stumble across that I can use with everything I play, not just the piece I'm practicing – I make a list of them, starting in the back of the book and working forward. (That way I can always find them.) My goals are written on a 3 x 5 card which I use as a bookmark, so they're always in front of me when I make my plan. And here and there I've taped in photographs of people who inspire me for one reason or another.

THREE THINGS TO DO BEFORE YOU PRACTICE

1. Show up.

"Eighty per cent of success is showing up." – Woody Allen

Practicing is a volunteer activity. We don't have to do it and, of course, most people choose not to.

But, unlike most people, we want to be pianists, or guitarists, or trumpeters, or drummers, or fiddlers. We say, "I want to play music," and we know that means "I want to practice." Playing comes from practicing, like cake comes from baking. Yo Yo Ma didn't become a great cellist because he bought a nice cello and then thought about it a lot. Larry Bird didn't become a great basketball player because he was tall. They both became great because they showed up to practice every day, whether they felt like it or not.

Practicing is the price of admission, the key to the treasure chest. It's the reason you can play and the guy next door can't. So you have to show up. You can't get better by thinking about it, or planning to do it, or doing it three days a week. That's like trying to swim without getting your hair wet, or trying to exercise without getting sweaty. You might as well not bother.

2. Set up.

There are things you will need every time you practice – things like:

- notebook
- metronome
- glass of water
- comfortable chair
- assignments list
- pencil & eraser
- music stand
- good lighting
- picks, rosin, reeds
- music books
- instrument stand
- glasses
- timer

Arrange all of these pieces of your practice area exactly the way you want them, before you start, every time. You may also want to close the door, arrange for someone else to get the phone (if you can) and go to the bathroom before you start. You may have some favorite object you like to have nearby when you practice, like a photo of a favorite musician. You may like the room warmer or cooler when you practice. There may be one time of day that's best for you to practice. *Whatever you can do to make your practice environment ideal for you, do it before you start, and do it every time.*

These days, when we say someone has genius, we mean they have great intelligence, skill, knowledge, and insight. But the word *genius* used to mean something very different. In ancient Rome, a "genius" was a spirit living in the walls of an artist's workshop who would come out when the time was right and help him do his work. The artist wasn't a genius; the artist *had* a genius. Saying he had a genius meant he had supernatural help *built into his work area.* Whether or not you believe in supernatural help for musicians, there's value in arranging your practice area so that it helps you do your work.

Practicing is different from everything else you do. It has its own rules and its own standards; it requires its own state of mind. There's nothing wrong with having a little ritual to get your mind into the right place for practicing. There's nothing wrong with creating your own personal world to practice in.

3. Warm up.

Musicians are small muscle athletes, and music is sport for the hands. You have to warm them up (arms, shoulders, neck, back, and breath, too – and legs and feet for drummers, organists, and people in marching bands.) Stretch a bit before you get started. Make the first few minutes of your practice session casual and easy, just to get the muscles moving and the blood flowing.

You also may need to warm up your head and ears. For the length of your practice session, whether it's twenty minutes or two hours, you'll need to postpone the rest of your life and focus on practicing. It doesn't happen automatically; use your warm-up time to shift mental gears. It may help to think of setting aside your daily thoughts, concerns and rituals, and picking up your practice thoughts, concerns, and rituals. Get into your mechanic's mindset.

I have a friend who puts on his Practice Hat. It's an actual hat – a well-worn New York Mets baseball cap – that he wears every time he practices, and only when he practices.

TWO THINGS TO DO AFTER YOU PRACTICE

1. Write it up.

Most days, if your practicing goes well, you'll learn a few things; maybe you'll have a breakthrough or an achievement. You may uncover something unexpected that needs work. Make sure you write all these things in your notebook so you don't forget them. Read through them again every day at the beginning of your session.

2. Pack up.

If you are lucky enough to have a practice area that you can leave set up all the time, then Packing Up may just be a matter of saying "Thank you" to the universe for the privilege of playing an instrument, and closing the door. If not, you'll have to put away your gear first and get your mind out of practice mode and back into day-to-day mode. Then, say "Thank you" and close the door.

NOT THE END

PRACTICING FOR A LIFETIME

I t's hard to play music your whole life. The world is not set up to allow you enough practice time. Friends who envy you for going to golf school or learning to skydive will think there's something wrong with you for taking piano lessons. And your family, no matter how much they love you, don't want to listen to you practice scales.

It's hard to maintain your passion, too. With time and exposure, passion cools to enthusiasm, then enjoyment, then familiarity, and finally nostalgia. (*"Hey, what was that song you used to play?"*)

Practicing takes work, energy and commitment. So do jobs, and so do families, and, of course, they come first.

But plenty of people find a way, as they have for hundreds of years. Obviously there are obstacles along the path; but, despite the fact that everyone's journey is different, the obstacles are very much the same from one journey to another. They can be sorted into three broad categories:

- Keeping your head on straight

- Finding the time

- Keeping Fresh

KEEPING YOUR HEAD ON STRAIGHT

For younger players and those who are just getting started, the concerns that most often arise are practical matters:

- How do I play that song?

- Where can I find a good teacher?

- What type of instrument should I buy?

For adults, trying to balance practicing with family and work obligations, the questions sooner or later become philosophical:

- How much better am I going to get at this?

- I'm never going to make any money playing music; why am I still doing it?

- What do I expect to accomplish?

- Do I want to spend all this time practicing instead of being with my family?

- How many more times can I play these same songs?

- Why am still doing this at my age?

Unfortunately, being an amateur musician is often seen as something to get out of your system when you're young. Adults can play golf or tennis, or watch football, and that's OK. But sing, or play in a band, or take lessons? "Aren't you a little old for that?"

The reasons for this odd prejudice don't matter, and our response to it is a simple one: Who cares? In the end, all these questions (and others like them) boil down to these two:

- Do I enjoy it?

- Is that enough?

The answers to the other questions may change all the time. As long as the answers to the last two are "Yes" and "Yes," you can forget about asking the others.

FINDING THE TIME

In day-to-day terms the biggest obstacle to a lifetime of practicing may be finding the time to do it. Every player finds his or her own solution to this problem. Of course, there aren't all that many different solutions to choose from. You can get up early, before everyone else, and practice first thing in the morning (my favorite). You can dedicate a set time in the evening, after work and dinner. You can take your instrument to work and practice at lunch hour. For most people, those are the choices. None is perfect; none works for everyone; none works all the time.

The key is consistency. Whatever time you pick, commit to it. If you're going to practice from 6:30 AM to 7:00 AM every day, do it every day. If you're trying out a schedule to see if it will work for you, commit to it for a month and then decide.

The good news is, finding the time is no more complicated than that. It's simple. Not easy, but simple.

KEEPING FRESH

If there is one secret to practicing for a lifetime, Keeping Fresh may be it. People quit because they think they don't have the time, or they get bored, or they're not getting anything out of it any more, or they're tired of it, or they just feel 'done'. It has gotten stale; the spice that attracted them in the first place is gone.

People who keep at it for a lifetime get stale, too, but they find ways to refresh themselves.

Time off: Sometimes it's as simple as stopping for a while. They take a week, a month, even a year off, during which they don't play at all, or play very little. When they come back to it, the instrument sounds different. Their hands feel different. Music sounds different. It's all fresh again.

New ears: One sure way to refresh your playing is to change the way you listen to music. You can go *deeper*, or you can go *broader*.

Listening deeper. Most of the music written over the last 500 years or so has multiple layers. Compositions have melodies, countermelodies, bass lines, variations, contrasting sections, and on and on. Most of us don't dig very far below the surface. We learn the melody and whatever part features our own instrument, and that's usually enough.

If you're getting stale, dig deeper. What's the bass doing? What are the horns doing? What's the drummer doing? If you had to describe it in words, what would you say? If you had to convince the drummer to play something different, what would you ask her to do?

Listening broader. If you get stale, spend some time listening to music, not because you like it, but because it's unfamiliar. Spend a month listening only to music you've never heard before. You may not love all of it, but it will change how you hear the music you do love.

Performance. There is one hard part that seems to appear in just about every song worth playing. The hard part is the last 10%, and it's a powerful cause of staleness.

We all recognize this scenario. There's one piece that you can never play perfectly. Maybe it has a single passage that you stumble over every time. Maybe you're never really sure, when you start this piece, that you're going to reach the end without getting lost. Maybe it just doesn't sound or feel right when you play it.

That piece sticks around on the music stand forever, never finished but never abandoned. You're 90% done with it, but you never get all the way. That last 10% is the hardest part.

It's hard for several reasons. One is that you're so-o-o-o-o close. The difference between 90% and 100% seems so small that it's easy to convince yourself it doesn't matter. Another reason is that whatever is wrong with the piece has probably been there from the very beginning, and you're used to it now. You've put in a reasonable amount of work on it, and it's still not right, so maybe it's good enough. Like a leaky faucet you've learned to live with, you've decided it doesn't really bother you. And, of course, if it was something you really wanted to work on, you would have done it by now.

All excuses, of course, and there's one more big one. When you practice, you are always dealing with things you can't play yet. *As long as you're practicing, it's ok for a piece to have mistakes in it.* That piece is going to stay in your practice rotation until it gets completely stale and you give up on it, having played it wrong for years and never once gotten it right. Do that often enough and you're practicing getting stale.

So, change from *practicing* to *playing*. Schedule a performance. Commit to yourself and an audience that the piece will be perfect by 8:00 PM a week from Friday. After all, as much as you enjoy practicing, your ultimate goal is not to practice; it's to play. Your performance can be for strangers, friends, family or an audience of one. Now you have a fresh set of problems to solve, requiring a different frame of mind. Plus, you have a deadline, which focuses the mind like nothing else.

Playing music with others. There's nothing like it. How much fun is shooting baskets by yourself, compared with playing a game of basketball? How much fun is speaking into a tape recorder, compared with having a conversation? How much fun is practicing dance steps, compared with dancing with someone else?

Like performing, playing with someone else requires you to prepare. An impending gig will force you to make decisions about what you can really play versus what you wish you could play. It will force you to think about your repertoire. Like performing, it pushes you out of the *practice* mindset into the *play* mindset.

Playing with someone else can provide you with fresh musical input. You will have to accommodate your playing to theirs, since, suddenly, there are two (or more) minds at work creating the music you're playing. You may also find that there are two (or more) sets of standards about what's correct and what's not, what's ready to play and what's not. It's a sociable way of allowing yourself to be nudged out of your comfort zone.

One more thing gets added by both performing and playing with others: adrenaline. It changes everything: how you hear, how you think, how you move, how you play. Adrenaline doesn't show up often in the practice room, but it's always there on stage.

Use the Force. There was something that brought you to music in the first place, some indescribable quality you can't get anywhere else. It doesn't automatically hang around waiting for you while you go to work. Go out and find it. Document it. Hoard it. Enjoy it. Remember it. Cherish it. Don't let it get away again.

CPSIA information can be obtained at www.ICGtesting.com
Printed in the USA
LVOW11s1006140515

438487LV00003B/71/P